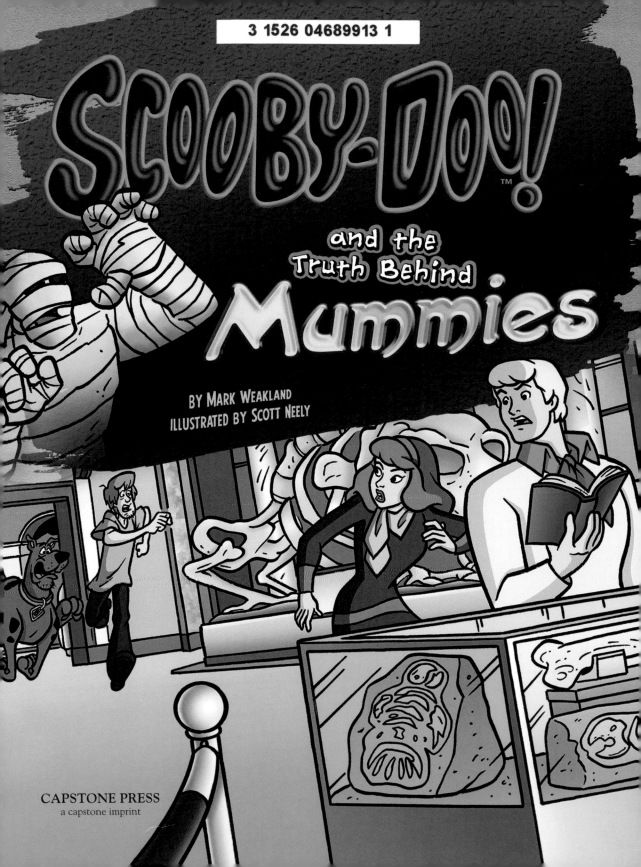

SCOOBY-DOO!™
and the Truth Behind
Mummies

BY MARK WEAKLAND
ILLUSTRATED BY SCOTT NEELY

CAPSTONE PRESS
a capstone imprint

Published in 2015 by Capstone Press,
A Capstone Imprint
1710 Roe Crest Drive
North Mankato, Minnesota 56003
www.capstonepub.com

CAPS32968

Library of Congress Cataloging-in-Publication Data
Weakland, Mark, author.
Scooby-Doo and the truth behind mummies /
by Mark Weakland ; illustrated by Scott Neely.
pages cm. —— (Unmasking monsters with Scooby-Doo)
Summary: "The popular Scooby-Doo and the Mystery Inc. gang
teach kids all about mummies"—— Provided by publisher.
Audience: Ages 6–8.
Audience: K to grade 3.
Includes bibliographical references and index.
ISBN 978-1-4914-1792-8 (library binding)
1. Mummies—Juvenile literature. 2. Monsters—Juvenile
literature. 3. Curiosities and wonders—Juvenile literature.
I. Neely, Scott, illustrator. II. Title. III. Title: Mummies.
GN293.W43 2015
001.944——dc23   2014029120

Editorial Credits:
Editor: Shelly Lyons
Designer: Ted Williams
Art Director: Nathan Gassman
Production Specialist: Tori Abraham

Design Elements:
Shutterstock: ailin1, AllAnd, hugolacasse, Studiojumpee

The illustrations in this book were created traditionally, with
digital coloring.

Thanks to our adviser for her expertise, research, and advice:
Elizabeth Tucker Gould, Professor
of English Binghamton University

Printed in the United States of America in
Stevens Point, Wisconsin
092014   008479WZS15

Scooby-Doo and the gang were visiting the museum. They were excited to see the new exhibits. But Scooby and Shaggy were nowhere to be found.

"This museum is so big," said Velma. "I hope they didn't get lost."

The quiet was broken when Shaggy and Scooby burst into the room. "Rummy!" barked Scooby.

"He thinks he saw a mummy!" yelped Shaggy. "In the Ancient Egypt room!"

"A human body," said Fred. "Ancient Egyptians removed the brain and other internal organs. They left the heart in place. Then the body was dried with a salt called natron and wrapped in linen."

"Why?" asked Scooby.

"To prepare it for the afterlife," said Velma.

"The brains were removed too," added Daphne. "But in stories or movies, mummies are smart, even without brains."

"Then the body was placed in a coffin. Sometimes the coffin was placed into a stone coffin called a sarcophagus," said Velma. "Then the sarcophagus was put into a tomb."

"How do we know if a mummy is chasing us?" asked Shaggy nervously.
"In movies mummies often moan," said Fred. "And shuffle their feet."

"Roaning and ruffling?" Scooby said.
"And a mummy is wrapped in cloth,"
said Velma. "That's a dead giveaway!"

"Yes," said Fred. "In movies and stories, mummies are very strong. And they carry a curse that affects those who disturb them. Sometimes they have special powers too."

"Some can move objects just by thinking. That's called telekinesis," said Velma.

"And some control insects, wind, or sand with their minds," added Daphne.

"Bugs!" yelled Shaggy.

"Yuck!" barked Scooby.

"You don't have to worry," said Daphne. "Legendary
mummies are strong, but they move slowly.

"Another way to protect yourself is with fire," said Fred.
"Mummies catch fire easily because of their wrappings.
If you set one on fire, it will be destroyed."

"Rokay!" said Scooby.

GLOSSARY

ancient—from a long time ago

internal organs—parts of the inside of the body; the heart, lungs, liver, and kidneys are organs

legend—a story handed down from earlier times; it is often based on fact, but is not entirely true

linen—cloth made from a flax plant

telekinesis—power to move things with the mind

tomb—a room or building that holds a dead body

READ MORE

Frisch, Aaron. *Mummies. That's Spooky!* Mankato, Minn.: Creative Education, 2013.

Sloan, Christopher. *Mummies: Dried, Tanned, Sealed, Drained, Frozen, Embalmed, Stuffed, Wrapped, and Smoked...and We're Dead Serious.* Washington, D.C.: National Geographic, 2010.

Biskup, Agnieszka. *Uncovering Mummies: An Isabel Soto Archaeology Adventure.* Graphic Expeditions. Mankato, Minn.: Capstone Press, 2010.

INTERNET SITES

FactHound offers a safe, fun way to find Internet sites related to this book. All of the sites on FactHound have been researched by our staff.

Here's all you do:

Visit *www.facthound.com*

Type in this code: 9781491417928

 Check out projects, games and lots more at **www.capstonekids.com**

INDEX